# My 20 years with Barbie

Advice Guide for Beginner  Collectors

# Table of contents:

# Introduction.

I remember my beginnings in the Barbie world, I felt so attracted by all that beauty concentrated in a doll. I just wanted to start knowing all the different models, collections… all them as soon as possible.

I jumped of into it thinking that in a few hours I would dominate all the Barbie collecting world. There was nothing further... it took me an eternity to update myself and have a slight idea of it.

And the thing is that every year it continues to grow more and more and more.

I'm currently working in a toy shop and many people comes daily to me asking for advice on the different editions, if there is one or another actress on the doll, how to get a better price... and it really surprises me when given the most basic advice it helps the costumer.

When friends or clients see my collection

they always think I have spent a little fortune on it. Believe me, nothing further, I have only observed the market and learned how to buy in the right moment and place.

Now, after 20 years, I acknowledge all the things I had unconsciously learned throughout all this time and have decided to create this little guide. Hope these advices, which are so logical to me because of experience, can serve the newcomers immerse into this magic  world and, maybe, even be useful for the more veterans.

I will not enter into details that usually appear in other guides such as the history about the doll or any other peculiarity that you can easily find on the Internet and that you probably already know. Nor have I added any type of photography, we all know how beautiful dolls are but accessing them is equally easy.

However, I have considered it convenient to use as a reference, in the examples of my classification, some of the dolls that have caught my attention in all these years.

Many of them are really beautiful but, as well, quite unknown to beginner collectors. One of the aims I have in mind when writing this little guide is to expand the beauty of Barbie world and made it more accessible to everyone.

All the information I share now is basically focused on my personal experience and everything I've learned through these 20 years of working on it.

I have also tried to be as brief as possible, I don't want to overwhelm the reader with a large amount of data, only the essential.

And now we are beginning the great adventure of showing you the beautiful world of Barbie.

# My first date with Barbie.

I think that from my earliest childhood I have known the doll, even in the early 70´s in Spain it was almost impossible to ignore her charm and glamour for the most sensitive to beauty.

I had a small inconvenience, being a boy and at that time, it was practically unthinkable I would have asked for a Barbie as a Christmas gift. But I always had plenty of creativity that helped me to circumvent my small-minded environment.

So, in my early eight years I gave my little sister, of only three, a Barbie Rockers as a present. Curiously nobody found it strange.

And that was my first contact with the doll. On those dull days, Barbie was like and anachronism which come from a far remoteness future. All my reality was sad grey and she was a complete full coloured rainbow.

And I continued growing up, too busy surviving,  time passed by and I completely forgot about her.

But a cold winter day walking through the covered and warm shopping center, I passed my gaze through the colorful showcase of a toy store …

… It is true the proverb that there are many things in live that will catch your eye but only a few will catch your heart.

And there she was, adapted to new times, in a Cleopatra costume and with one of the most beautiful face, that until then, I had only seen in movies, Elizabeth Taylor.

And that it´s my number one, I still have it in her showcase, like Uncle Scrooge with his first coin, untouchable, just for me.

Many years have passed by and I have changed in many aspects, but luckily, I have never lost the ability to enjoy things as I did when I was a child. And so I continue, a man of many years with the passion, not understandable for everyone, to collect dolls.

# Placing a little order.

Mattel is continually releasing new dolls to market so it is quite understandable how confusing may seem to the beginner to start a first approach to all differents editions, collections…

In my experience, the first useful classification we must take into account is the year in which the edition was launched.

It is not, for example, the same doll a Barbie Scarlett O'Hara edition of 1996 than the others who were launched in the future 2001 and 2008, much more elaborated and faithful to the actress.

Similarly, the prices vary from one edition to another. (Later I will address the issue of so dissimilar prices and how to orient ourselves best in the market).

The same goes for other types of collections, there are a range list of barbies, specially those from movies, that has many differents editions.

In my beginnings,  Barbie website was not so elaborated, only listing last editions never oldest  ones. But actually, I can assure it is the best reference you can find online

https://barbie.mattel.com.

Just entering the web and typing the name of the doll, current or old, you will see all the editions and the year they came out. There is nothing simpler.

Another interesting classification from Mattel to be considered is the number of copies of each edition. Currently, the used labels are.

**Pink Label** - It is distributed nationwide, there is no limit, and there may be reissued in the same year if there is a lot of demand.

**Silver Label** - Less than 50,000 units worldwide.

**Gold label** - Less than 10,000 units worldwide.

**Platinum Label** - Less than 1,000 units worldwide.

**Black Label** - The last to arrive and a bit confusing because it does not specify the number of manufactured units. Some people place it between Pink and Silver.

It is important to bear in mind that before the Barbie boom there were many other collections on the market that usually appeared as Collector's Edition, although there is no data on the number of dolls in each edition.

Normally, to differentiate a collectors edition from a more common one (apart from labels) it is very useful to look at the box they come in, since they are made for the exhibition and tend to be much more elegant and elaborated.

Important to remark that I have seen really beautiful dolls with spectacular costumes but they are not collectible despite being beautiful dolls, search online for "Barbie Secret of the Three Teardrops" and you will understand me.

In case of doubt, just enter the usual official website, look for the name in their search engine and if it does not appear it is simply not a collectable one. In spite of this, if it is s beautiful doll you should not deprive yourself of getting it. They are still rare because they are vintage and they are usually much cheaper than the official ones.

Another fact I have noticed is that, just as all Barbies are not collectibles, all of Mattel's dolls are not Barbie. Again, many collectors do not take this into account and simply choose the doll because they like it, it does not matter if it belongs to one classification or another but if you prefer to limit your collection to the authentic collections, before deciding, as always, look on the official page.

Other Mattel classifications that you may find useful are:

**Barbie Fan Club** - Those distributed through Barbie's club members, in theory, was the only way to get them unless a collector place theirs on sale. Currently, they are very easy to obtain thanks to the second-hand market.

**Limited Edition** - Limited to less than 35,000 units.

**Timeless Treasures**. - Edition with myths like Frank Sinatra, Cher, Marilyn Monroe, the 2001 edition of Gone With the Wind, Barbie Lucy episode Be a Pal and James Dean.

**Direct Exclusive** - Those that can only be purchased by ordering online on the Barbie website.

Important  to point out that there are other stores, online or not, that  had their exclusive Barbie distributed only through their stores. So we have the Fao Schwarz and Spiegel (two American department stores) or even recently Amazon. I strongly recommend these dolls, not only are beautiful but quite undervalued.


**<u>Treasure Hunter</u>** - One of my favorites for the unusual, although in reality only two models of this category were released.

It could be called the beginning of the Barbie Platinum Label, the same doll model but with a slight variation, a different color suit or a different necklace.

They look the same but they are not, search online for "Exotic Beauty Barbie" and the same model but adding "Treasure Hunter" and you will understand. The other is the Corvette, much easier to detect by the pink color of the suit.

# And now our own classification.

I repeat this  is something unique to us and we hope it will serve you as it helped us to put some order in all the different models we have on display.

## 1.- Cinema, TV Series, Singers and Stars of the Classic Hollywood.

They are usually the most sought after, simply because they belong to "crossed collecting". They are pursued by both Barbie collectors and those who are fans from the series, actress or film they represent.

Aside I must admit that they are becoming more perfect and similar to the original with every new edition, so quite understandable they are so acclaimed.

Some examples:

- Gone with the Wind (3 editions, 1996, 2001 and recently 2014)
- My Fair Lady (1,996, 4 Eliza Doolittle and 1 professor Higgins)
- Grease (10 different models, no Kens in this collection)
- Twilight (8 Barbies, 6 Kens and one set with both Bella and Edward)
- Hunger Games (4 Barbies and 4 Kens)
- Divergent (2 Barbies and 1 Ken)
- Lord of the Rings (2001) (Galadriel, Legolas, and a set with Arwen and Aragorn)
- Star Trek (the first set came out in 1996 with Barbie and Ken together, in my opinion one of the most undervalued in history, selling at a quite low prices)
- James Bond (5 Barbies and one set with Barbie and Ken)
- X-Files (in the 1998 edition set, you will find two different versions, the Scully doll with long hair, that the actress did withdrawn from sale, not liking the result, and the one that was finally marketed with  the shorter

hair)

*The series of classic actors and actresses,*

- Marilyn Monroe (3 dolls in 1997, and one in 2001, 2002 and 2009)
- Elvis Presley (6 Ken dolls and two sets, one with Barbie and another in wedding suit with Priscilla)
- Frank Sinatra (1 Ken doll, 1 set with Barbie and one Barbie  characterized as the singer)
- Grace Kelly (4 dolls of which 2 are silkstone)
- Audrey Hepburn (4 dolls of witch 1 is silkstone)
- Elizabeth Taylor *(5 dolls of which 2 are silkstone)*
- Rod Hudson with Doris Day (Pillow Talk)
- Tippi Hedren (The Birds by Alfred Hitchcock's)
- The Munsters
- Family Addams

*Characters of movies and series,*

- Rose  (Titanic)
- Elle (Legally Blonde 2)
- King Kong
- I Love Lucy (american TV series of the 50, almost every year one goes on sale, actually 20 different ones released)
- Dynasty (both Krystle and Alexis)
- That Girl (american TV series of the 60s)
- Farrah Fawcett (Charlie's Angels)


***And some celebrities like,***


- Goldie Hawn
- Barbra Streisand
- Cher (4 editions, one platinum label)
- Jennifer Lopez (2 editions)
- Cindy Lauper
- Heidi Klum
- Debbie Harry
- Joan Jett
- Diana Ross

# 2.- Designers and Fashion World.

Naming them all would be an almost impossible task, highlighting Bob Mackie, the undisputed star in the Barbie world, and more:

Some more designers:

- Byron Lars (16 different models)
- Versace
    - Judith Lieber
    - Dior
    - Moschino
    - Zac Posen
    - Kimora Lee
    - Anna Sui
    - Cynthia Rowley
    - Tarina Tarantino
    - Vera Wang
    - Escada
    - Badgley Mischka
    - Christian Louboutin (3 models)
    - Diane Von Furstenberg
    - Oscar de la Renta (2 models)
    - Balenciaga (The first collectible Barbie in

Spain)
- Philipp Plein
- Carolina Herrera

# 3.- Fantasy.

Personally,  one of my favorites lines, goddesses, fairies, bride zombies, ghost ... I encourage you to discover them, each one it is a beautiful surprise.

Some examples of the least known:

- Aine
- Merlin and Morgan Le Fay
- Fairy of the Garden
- Arabian Nights
- Goddess of Spring
- Whispering Wind
- The Bard
- Faerie Queen
- Aphrodite
- Athena
- Jellyfish
- Countess Dracula
- Vampire
- Lady of the Unicorns

# 4.- Dolls of the World.

All the Mattel dolls released representing different countries, usually vary the name of the collection (Princesses, World Barbies, Barbies of the World, Passport Edition ...) but being of Pink Label have a large print and usually they reappear every few years reinvented.

Some examples of the least known:

- Irish Dance
- Princess of the French Court
- Princess of the Nile
- Princess of the Vikings
- Passport France
- Princess of the Incas
- Princess of South Africa
- Passport England

And of course a lot of countries:

- England

- Ireland
- Germany
- India
- Korea
- France
- Spain
- Italy
- Holland
- Greece
- Denmark

# 5.- Reproductions.

They are real gems of collecting for classic lovers. They are exact copies of the originals, but current editions and more affordable.

The box, the content, the face of the doll... everything identical. Luckily, every year many are reissued.

Some examples that you will love:

- Swirl Ponytail
- Student Teacher
- Astronaut
- Bubble Cut
- Campus Spirit Set
- Set Friday Night Dream Date
- Campus Sweetheart
- My Favorite Ken 1969
- Double Date
- Barbie and the Rockers
- Barbie Learns to Cook
- All That Jazz
- Campus Sweetheart
- Enchanted Evening

- Bowling Champ
- Superstar
- Poodle Parade
- Gay Parisienne
- Evening Gala
- Commuter Set
- Silken Flame
- Fashion Luncheon

## 6.- Silkstone.

Similar to the previous in the classic style but in  a classic covered cartoon box that does not let you see the doll if you do not open it. They usually goes with an inner wrapping of white silk paper.

They are named for the material they are made of, a kind of porcelain but stronger. The ones that usually make this type are dressed with quite elegant classic dresses or suits (Kens too allowed in this line).

Sometimes they also include some actress like Grace Kelly, Audrey Hepburn, Elizabeth Taylor or Vivien Leigh.
Some examples:

- Boater Ensemble
- Cocktail Dress
- Darya
- Nicolai
- Party Dress
- Gala Gown

- The Waitress
- The Lingerie collection (underwear)
- Mermaid Gown
- Lisette
- Eternal
- The Mad Men collection (current television series set in the 50s)
- The French Maid
- Southern Belle
- Stolen Magic

## 7.- Porcelain.

Not a very large collection, released mainly in the 90´s, always wrapped in very large boxes of cardboard with the inside of cork to avoid breakage.

Curiously, except for the Fabergés, they do not usually reach a high value in the market.


Some examples:


- Royal Splendor
- Fabergé series (3 different dolls, for the youngest, Fabergé was the jeweler of the Tsar's royal family in Russia, creator of the famous Fabergé eggs)
- Gold Sensation
- Crystal Rhapsody
- Holiday Ball
- Solo in the Spotlight
- Blushing Orchid Bride
- Plantation Belle
- Star Lily Bride

- Mint Memories
- Silver Starlight
- Gold Sensation
- Evening Pearl
- Romantic Rose
- Wedding Party
- Sophisticated Lady
- The Tango
- Charleston
- Classic Grace
- Lighter Than Air
- Orange Pekoe

# 8.- Historical Costumes.

Here we include from the spectacular Queen Marie Antoinette to those of the history of fashion (Great Fashions of 20th Century) or those of different eras (Great Eras Collection).

Some examples that you will love:

- Pop Life Collection (3 Barbies and one Ken platinum label set in the fabulous 60)
- Fabulous Forties
- Colonial
- Pioneer
- Venetian Opulence
- Grecian Goddess
- Museum Collection (Van Gogh, Da Vinci and Gustav Klimt)
- Lavinia
- Madame du Barbie
- Portrait Collection (3 different Barbies framed in a vintage looking cardboard box: Mademoiselle Isabelle, Emma Duchess and Lady Camille)
- Royal Jewels Collection (4 dolls with

authentic Swarovski crystals: Duchess of
Diamonds, Empress of Emeralds,
Countess of Rubies and Queen of
Sapphires)
- Wedgwood Collection (2 different, one blue
and one pink, with real necklaces from the
famous English porcelain house)
- Empress Sissy

# 9.- Basics.

This is perhaps the most confusing when it comes to classifying it but once understood it is quite simple. They are collections of basic fashion, in transparent boxes smaller than usual, like a small urn, and very easy to identify.

They all carry the word Basic and are classified by numbers, the number that carries two zeros at the beginning is the season number , there are 4 so far and they are:

- **001**   (12 different models)
- **001,5** (4 different models)
- **002**   (9 barbie models and 3 ken)
- **003**   (6 different models, all bikinis and swimsuits)

The number that carries a zero ahead is the model number within that season. For example the 04, 003, refers to the model number 4 of the third season. It may seem a bit confusing but with pictures in sight it is much easier to identify them.

Some examples:

No 05, collection 002
No 04, collection 001
No 04, collection 003
No 15, collection 002

# 10.- Ballet.

They may be less models in this section but they are also very interesting and they deserve their own place.

Some examples:

- Ballet Wishes Series (6 different)
- Classic Ballet Series (10 different)
- Swan Lake
- Nutcracker Collection (the current Disney movie 4 different)
- Prima Ballerina Collection (in porcelain, two different, highly sought after and consequently of high price)

# 11.- Comics.

This is one of the sections where you can find more variant versions of the same character, the record is taken by Wonder Woman, since it includes the first versions of Mattel and the latest versions of films like Superman Vs Batman, Paradise Island and others. In total we already count with 6 varying dolls.


Other examples in this section:

- Batman (2 Kens, 3 Catwoman and a Batgirl)
- Superman (2 Kens, 1 Barbie Louise and another      Batgirl)
- Black Canary
- Harley Quinn
- Electra
- Poison Evy
- Fantastic 4

# 12.- Christmas

They are usually of more striking boxes, you can find from the first of Happy Holidays until the last of this year. per usual  taking out more than one release each new holiday season.
We would also include here the specials such as the 2000 or the victorian holiday. The spectrum is also very broad and always following the central theme of Christmas.


More examples:

- Happy Holidays series (the oldest, from 1988 to 1988) - Holiday Barbie Collection (2004 to present)
- Victorian Holiday Barbie and Kelly
- Victorian Holiday Fan Club
- Holiday Traditions
- Victorian Holiday with Cedric Bear
- Holiday Memories
- Celebration 2000

# 13.- Disney and Children´s.

From Little Red Riding Hood and the Wolf, the Flintstones, the classics such as Beauty and the Beast, Mickey and Minnie, Beatrix Potter …

The most complicated to differentiate are Disney ones, versions of for example, Sleeping Beauty manufactured by Mattel there are several but only one is Barbie.

The most certainly repeated characters are those from The Wizard of Oz, up to 22 different Barbies (Dorothy, Glinda, Wicked Witch of the East, Wicked Witch of the West) and 15 Ken (Scarecrow, Cowardly Lion, Tin Man and a Winkie Guard)

Some examples:

- Mary Poppins (3 Barbies, two different Kens)
- A Sprinkle in Time (3 different characters)
- Snow White
- Sleeping Beauty
- Cinderella

- Beauty and the Beast Barbie
- Rapunzel
- Little Bo Peep
 - Little Red Riding Hood and the Wolf

# 14.- Commercial.

We can include in this section all the Barbies that different companies have decided to launch using it´s business name.  Quite original since they always follow the aesthetics of the company.

Some examples:

- Harley Davidson (7 Barbies, 2 Kens and a set with both)
- Hard Rock Café (8 different)
- Ferrari (3 different)
- Coca Cola (7 Barbies, a Ken and a Santa Claus)
- Nascar (4 different)
- North American Universities (Each one with her cheerleader barbie, lately also Ken)
- Mac Cosmetics
- Chocolate Hamleys
- John Deere (tractors)

# 15.- Platinum Label.

Here we have chosen the same Mattel classification, no more than 1000 units worldwide. All could enter any other section but deserve a special mention for the uniqueness.

There are many platinum that are beautiful but for example they differ from a gold edition (much more affordable) for minor details such as hair color.

I advise those that are completely different and do not have other similar editions. Obvious to say how difficult they are to find.

Some examples:

- Judith Lieber
- Cher Ringmaster
- Karl Lagerfeld
- Andy Warhol
- The Reine de la Nuit
- Joie de Vivre
- Spring Break 1961

# 16.- Convention

Increasingly, there are collectors who decide to organize every year a convention where all the attendees have included in the price the entrance an exclusive Barbie made for that event.

Normally also less than 1000. This originally started in the US obviously, but lately it is beginning to expand also in Europe and we already have an annual convention in France, Spain and Italy. Of course the models vary according to the importance of the event.

Some examples,

- Masquerade 2005
- Lady Lion 2018
- Midnight Celebration 2014
- Passport to Pink 2012
- Joie de Vivre 2008
- Barbie in the Old West 2000
- Queen of the Prom 2001

- La Belle Epoque 2012
- Spotlight on Broadway 2015
- La Reine de la Nuit 2013
- Spring Break Set 2011
- Diva of the Nile 2007
- Lady Navy 2016

# 17.- OOAK.

They are the abbreviations of "One of a Kind" those dolls with a base of another Barbie model but completely retouched and completely reinvented as a new model.

Some are real beauties, as much by the dresses, the design and the faces. Of course, we all have an artist inside and I too made my own designs but nothing to do with the real pieces of art that some artist have the ability to create.

Remember this is our classification to put a bit of order when cataloging them. You can also create your own method whenever it's easier for you. Certainly, there are some that can belong to two or even more categories, for example, the Scarlett O'Hara silkstone of 2014 could be classified in the categories:

1 (classic Hollywood),
6 (Silkstone)
8 (Historical Costumes)


I encourage you to search internet for some names that I have included, they are really beautiful dolls and it is the best way to learn.

With time and after many seen dolls you will unconsciously classify and evaluate them without noticing.

# Where to get them and at the best price.

First of all, clarify that there are many price guides in the market but, in my opinion, they are usually obsolete since it is practically impossible to keep them up to date taking into account the speed of this market.

To have a more accurate barometer of prices, you should first consult the above-mentioned Barbie website and some online sales platforms.

Ideally, you should start buying the last ones at the right moment, do not buy them when they have just been launched, except buying directly from the Barbie website.

In my experience, when buying first units through internet before been listed in Mattel shop, when nobody has them, you pay quite expensive the exclusivity to be the first to own them.

It is also advisable to buy them in stores and always those of that year to avoid increases in the price.

# Different prices for the same model.

This is one of the things that intrigues most first time collectors, I will try to explain it as simple as possible.

The collection barbies are limited units, when selling units are finished, there are no more. Then it is when we have to resort to the secondary market and it is when confusion comes.

I recommend that you always use the search engine and logically buy the most economical, there are many people who do not know the value of the doll and simply puts a higher price, others, just the opposite. Although usually  online auction platforms informs you of the average price.

It is also highly advisable to buy first those you like most and are more sought after, since logically the longer you wait the more they will go up in value, some at really alarming prices.

In my experience, the ones that always tend to reach higher prices are those of classic actresses, Audrey Hepburn, Grace Kelly… Just the same with famous movies, Flashdance, The Birds...

# Buying in the US from another country.

Not all collectible barbies are available in all countries, sometimes only the most commercial ones arrive in Europe or any other part of the world.

And, from my sad experience, that particular doll that has stolen your heart, it is only available buying directly from the USA.

It is important if you decide to bring it directly, take into account the shipping costs. I always advise that you ask the seller to manufacture it as a certified letter but this it is only available when the doll it is not too heavy and does not take up much of  space.
It has the disadvantage that it can take up to two months to arrive, but sometimes with a little luck, in less than a month you have it at home.

The difference price in shipping from

EEUU could be between $25 as a registered letter to easily exceed $100 euros. Although even taking more than a week to arrive, it can rarely go below $50.

It is important to consider customs duties, many platforms like Amazon manage this payment, as well as shipping, in a global scale so it is quite more economic.                Always choose, when available, this option with all payments included to avoid surprises.

We know cases of collectors who have bought a $16 doll, choose to receive it as a registered letter and, when received, find the surprise of a customs letter asking for documentation, receives etc…  And after waiting another month, when lucky, having to pay the customs fee plus a 35 euros bill for documentation management.

Luckily, global trade is becoming more widespread every day and new methods are emerging that cheaper prices.

# Basic tips to get good prices on eBay or Amazon.

There are some small useful tips, but all based on having a little time  and knowing how to use cleverly the search engine.

Many people who usually decides to sell their dolls do not have the slightest idea of their value, or simply do not have the time to look for it. After all, for many sellers, it is only a doll.

So, sometimes,  it is useful in the search engine to choose the classify option  "latest for sale". With a little luck we can get amazing bargains before the others.

Another interesting method would be just the opposite, classify them by "first to finalize" and choose the auction option.

Some Barbies starts bidding at a really low price, even with only 1 euro. USA is a very large country with different time slots. It can happen that a novice salesman does not take this into account and his auctions end at a time when the vast majority of the population is already in bed. But that can coincidentally be a good time in Europe or Japan, for example.

Regarding the classification of the doll condition it  is quite simple.

NRFB is the most sought after, which is integrated into its box that has never been opened. The other classifications tend to be less used, there are some that have been exposed and then put back in their box and then, of course, those that come without a box.

But this is usually indicated in the ad without resorting to abbreviations since the seller makes a very clear description to avoid possible disappointments when receiving it.

Another tip that I give is that if you like to expose them out of their box, buy them directly deboxed if possible.

A lot of collectors are very careful people, you will get the doll practically new, much cheaper and you will save a lot on shipping costs and customs duties.

It is also important, as always before buying, to watch carefully pictures and read the entire description of the product.

# Conservation of doll and outside box.

Over time, as careful as you can be, doll's box may end up aging or not looking as nice and new as the first day.

One precaution we take is that as soon as we receive them we wrap all our dolls  in transparent plastic. We use a thicker than normal issue and that prevents the box suffer the least. You continue to admire the beauty of your doll and, at the same time, keep it completely intact.

You  can easily find this product online or even at your local florist store, it is same plastic they use for bouquet flowers.

Those dolls that come with the price tag, there is a way to remove it, a little risky although and needed of experience, you need to be very careful.

Just use  a lighter to heat it and get the

glue off so it will easily detached. It is complicated and requires practice,  when in doubt, keep the label for later times when you will feel more experienced.

There are collectors, the most practised ones, that use an iron but it is quite risky and only can be done when the label is on cardboard, never use when plastic.

Always caution, better a box with a label that one with the transparent cover melted or worse.

As for the way of showing them, I highly recommend crystal showcases, but such a beauty always finds a way to be exhibited, no matter where, they will always enhance any corner of the house.

When, lacking space, if you accumulate them in cabinets, be careful not to put the most fragile box underneath, since the weight will eventually deform.

# Create your own models.

This it is a great advice for young people or others, like me, that have plenty of time but not too much money  to spend. Or other  many collectors with a great imagination that are not patience to wait for the newest doll release.

You can create authentic wonders with very little budget and dedication, just a little time and imagination.
We offer you some ideas.

Renew the costumes of the Barbies with famous faces. You can get any barbie Elizabeth Taylor, Cher, Vivien Leigh ... and dress them in different costumes from other Barbies lines, occasionally , costumes are sold loose and so much more cheaper.

How would Elizabeth Taylor have looked in the role of Scarlett O'Hara? you only have to change the suit. Or Cher in a Dior design? Or Marilyn Monroe? The possibilities are endless.

Other collectors are also very good at making miniature costumes adapted to Barbie, here also the limit is your own imagination.

Another option is to use costumes from previous editions of Barbie but with the face of the old doll and change them to more current models, which you can get cheaper. The change is also spectacular.

A little secret for those who like to create their own designs. I do not recommend using gel or spray hair to stylish the doll, there is other option that is the styling water, which works really well, the hairstyle is defined and it looks like new from factory.

There are also those who enjoy creating the environment of the doll,  designing their own dioramas, from a living room to, the most handy, developing a whole Barbie mansion.

To get the necessary elements you do not need to spend a lot, sometimes a fridge magnet, key rings or small objects work perfectly and are in line with the scale of the doll to recreate these mini spaces.


    And finally we leave you  our website of our store/museum, we hope you enjoy it. Please, any questions you have, do not hesitate to write, we will be more than happy to help.


    suigenerishop@hotmail.com
www.SuiGenerisElche.com


    And here ends our little guide of advice, we really hope it has been helpful and I can only wish you a lot of happiness with our beloved Barbie